I0408321

LOVE, LACE & LINGERIE

ADULT COLORING BOOK

ASSEMBLED BY
MADDIE MAYFAIR

© March 2017

All rights reserved.

ISBN-13: 978-1545092149

ISBN-10: 1545092141

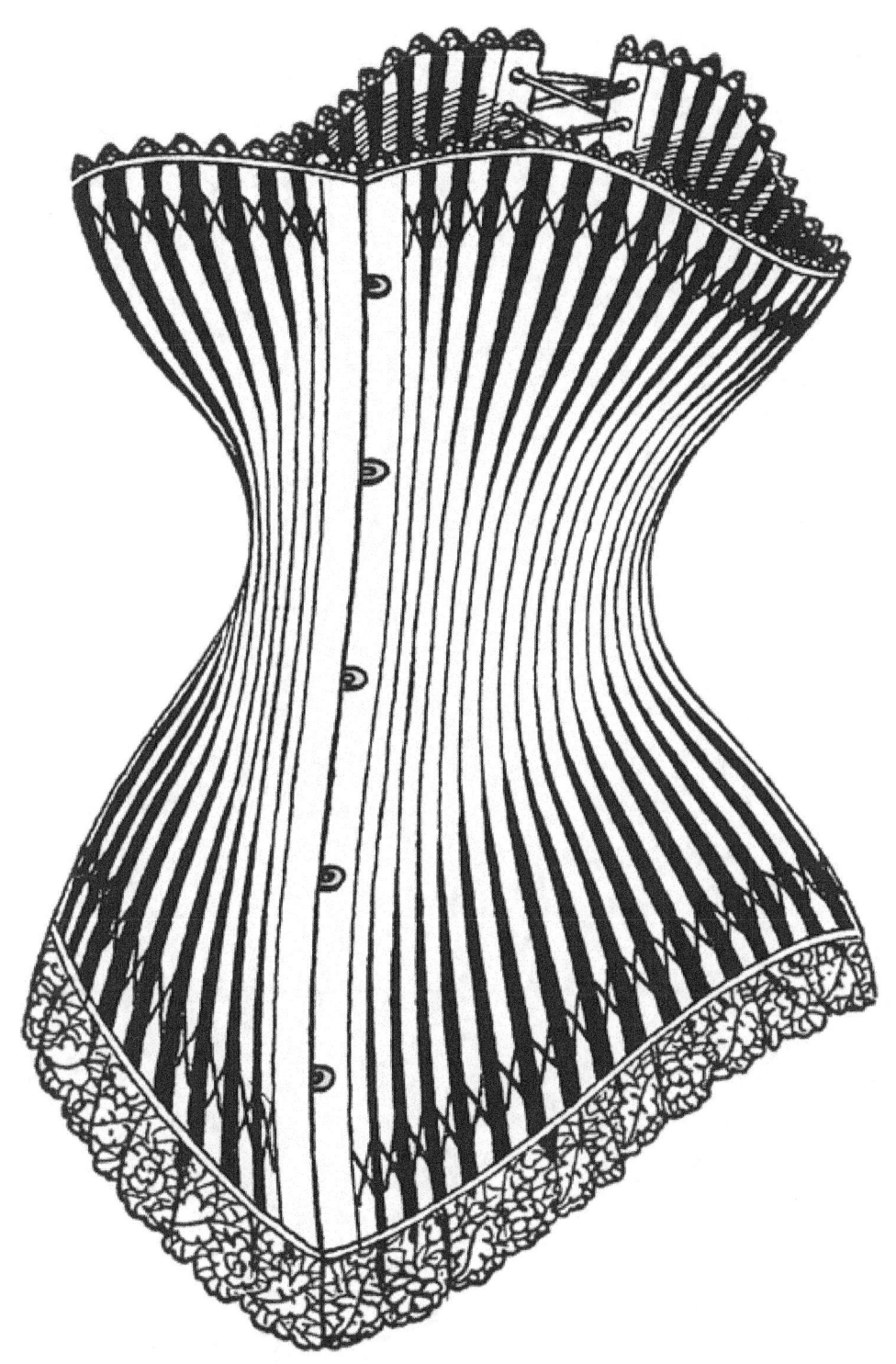

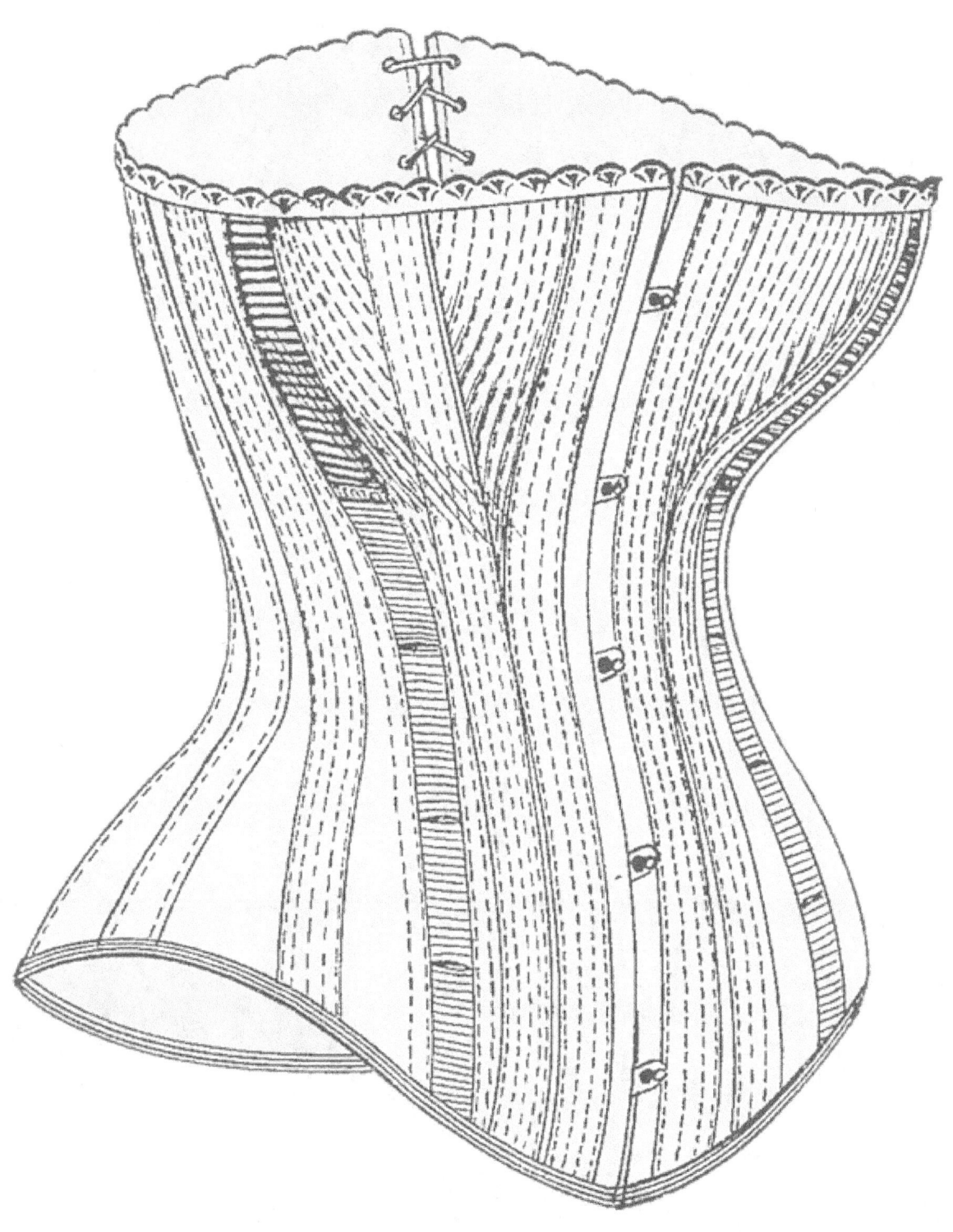

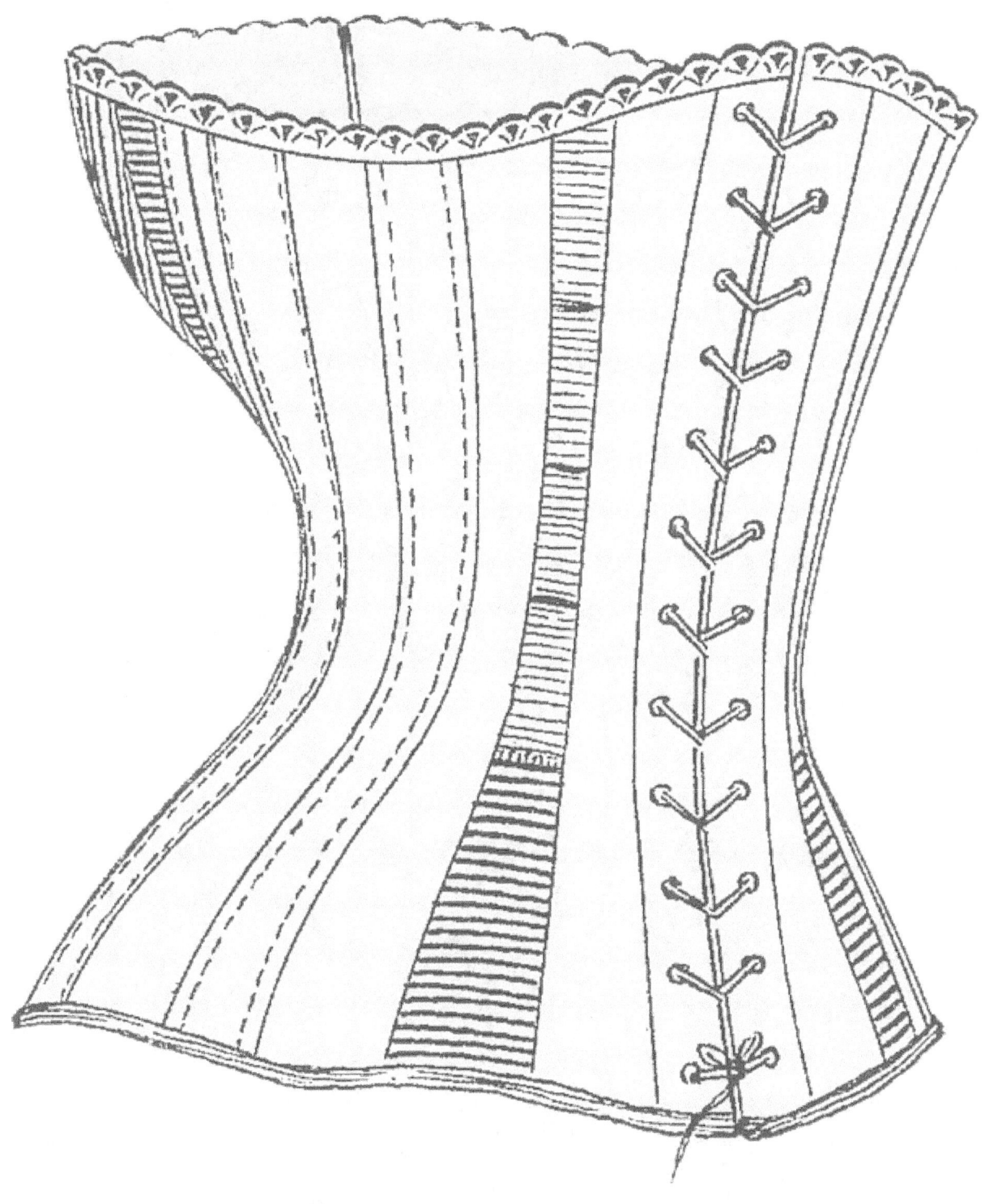

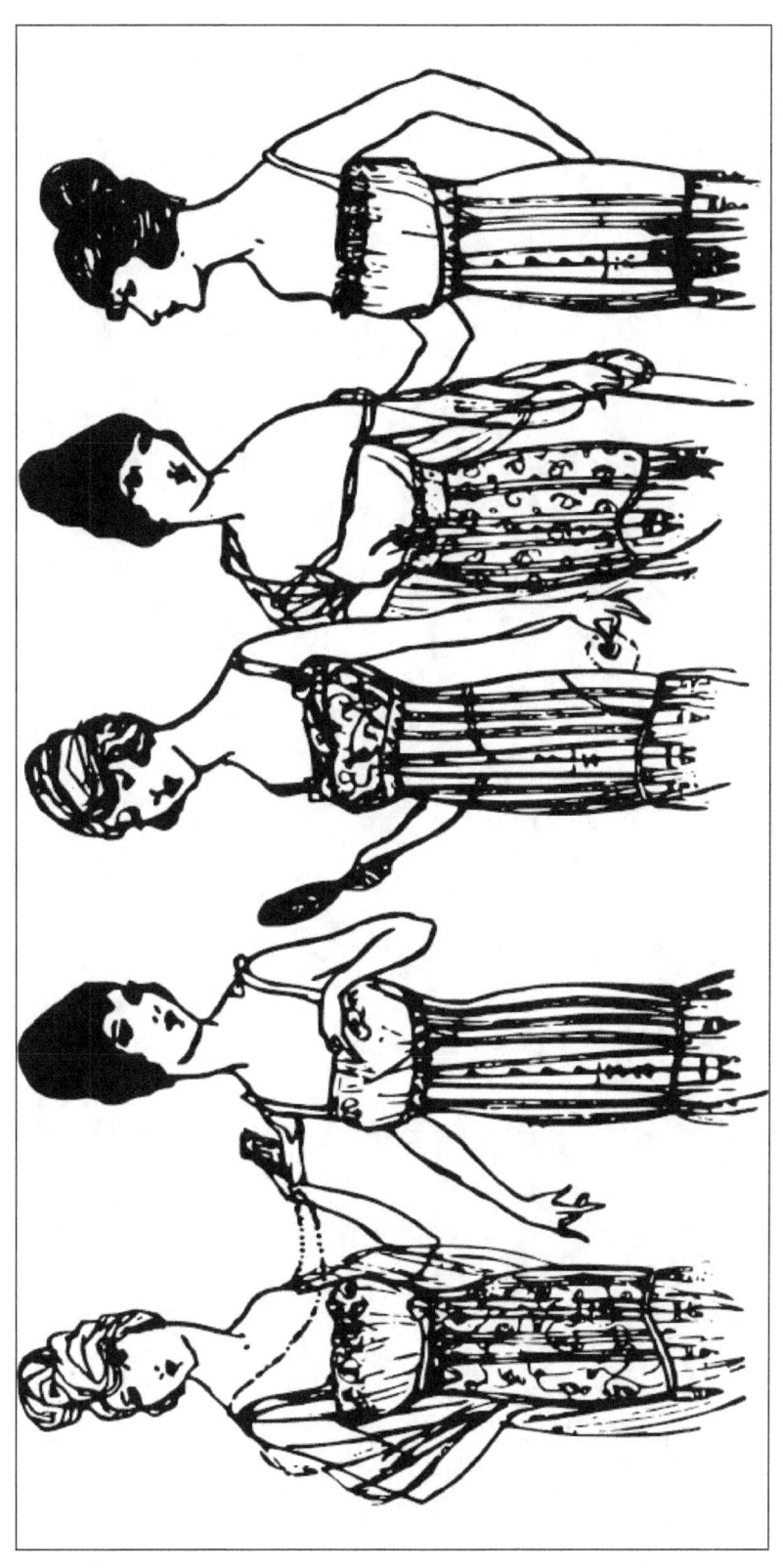

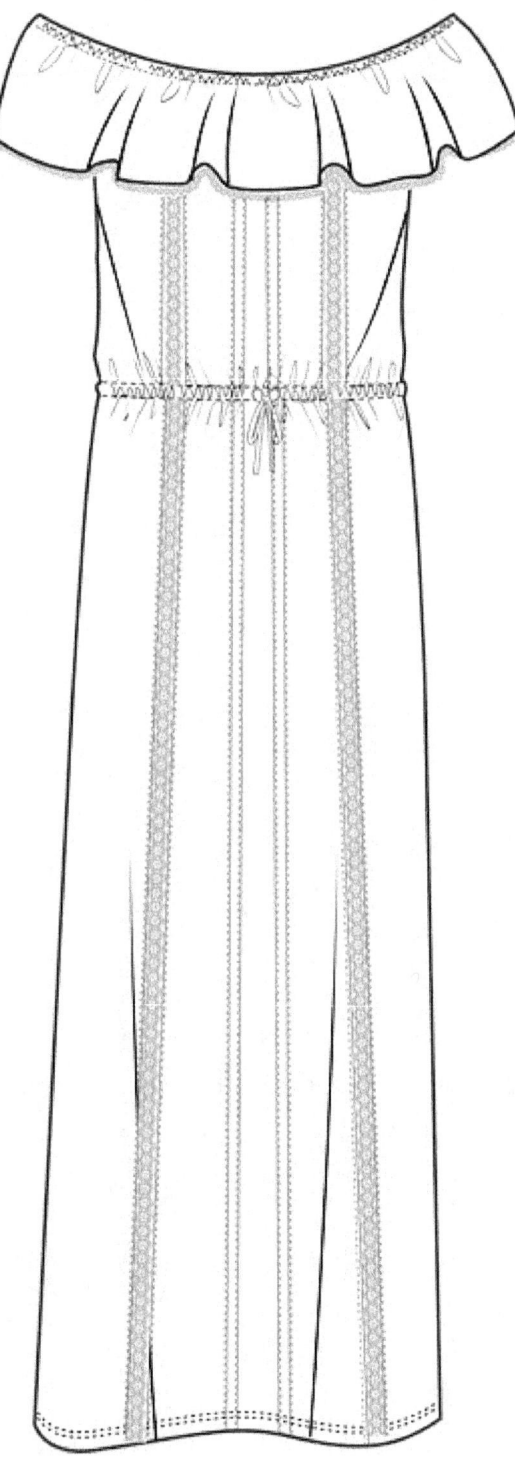

Enjoy even more *Colouring Books for Grown-Ups,* including:

www.ingramcontent.com/pod-product-compliance
Lightning Source LLC
Chambersburg PA
CBHW081427280526
45788CB00009B/3247